COMMUNITY HELPERS

POLICE

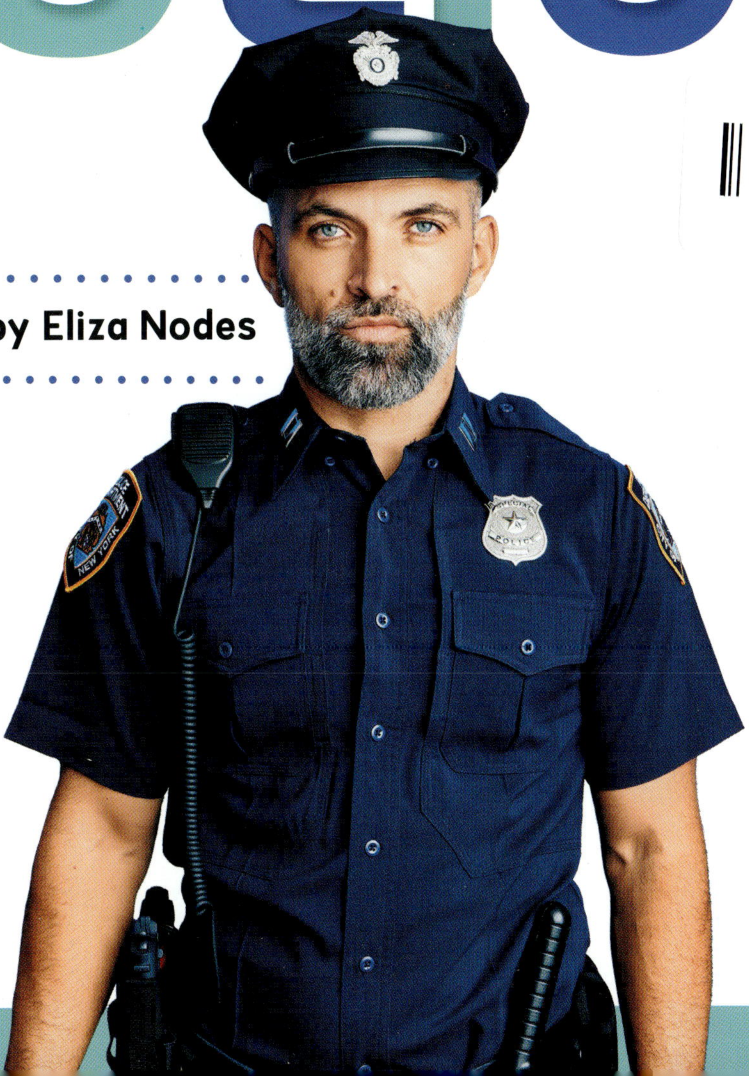

I0816203

Written by Eliza Nodes

This edition is published by arrangement with BookLife Publishing

sales@northstareditions.com | 888-417-0195

Library of Congress Control Number:
The Library of Congress Control Number is available on the Library of Congress website.

ISBN
979-8-89471-052-5 (library bound)
979-8-89471-072-3 (paperback)
979-8-89471-111-9 (epub)
979-8-89471-092-1 (hosted ebook)

Printed in the United States of America
Mankato, MN
012026

Written by:
Eliza Nodes

Edited by:
Rebecca Phillips-Bartlett

Designed by:
Ker Ker Lee

All facts, statistics, web addresses, and URLs in this book were verified as valid and accurate at time of writing. No responsibility for any changes to external websites or references can be accepted by either the author or publisher.

Photo Credits – Images courtesy of Shutterstock.com, unless otherwise stated.

Cover – Anutr Yossundara, 4kclips, puha dorin, SolidMak, Veronica Louro, SN VFX, xiaorui, Sean Locke Photography, Axstokes, Juiced Up Media, Peter Sobolev, Krakenimages.com, Grushin, SolidMaks. 2–3 – Pixel-Shot, Matt Gush. 4–5 – ilikeyellow, Sean Locke Photography. 6–7 – Princess_Anmitsu, Robert Kneschke, Ann Kosolapova. 8–9 – Andrey_Kuzmin, Gorodenkoff, RTimages, Wirestock Creators. 10–11 – Freaktography, Maxim Vasiliev, iaginzburg, pp1. 12–13 – Vereshchagin Dmitry, Krakenimages.com, xiaorui, n_defender. 14–15 – aperturesound, Juiced Up Media. 16–17 – cornfield, Hein Nouwens, William Barton, Nerthuz, New Africa. 18–19 – VGstockstudio, Richard Thornton. 20–21 – Kuznetsov Alexey, Juan Manuel Rodriguez, Andrey_Kuzmin, Victor Velter. 22–23 – Roman Samborskyi, LifetimeStock, Sean Locke Photography, Krakenimages.com, Raul Mellado Ortiz.

CONTENTS

Words that look like this can be found in the glossary on page 24.

POLICE OFFICERS

When you think of a police officer, what comes to mind?

Do you see someone wearing a uniform and a police badge? Do you hear the siren of a police car?

Police officers are important members of the community. They help keep people safe.

Police officers make sure people follow the law. Laws are sets of rules that everyone must follow. Laws keep communities safe and fair. Breaking the law is called committing a crime.

DID YOU KNOW?

People who break the law are called criminals.

MANY JOBS IN ONE

Police officers do many different jobs.

PATROLLING THE AREA

Police officers often patrol, or guard, an area. They may walk around. Sometimes they patrol in a car.

RESPONDING TO CALLS

People call the police after a crime. Then police officers respond. They go to the place the call came from.

OLLECTING STATEMENTS

eople who saw a crime re called witnesses. Police fficers ask them what they aw. These statements can elp solve crimes.

INTERVIEWING SUSPECTS

A suspect is someone who the police think may have broken the law. Police officers interview them to find out if they did.

COLLECTING EVIDENCE

Evidence is information the police collect. It is used to prove if something happened. It can include statements, interviews, or fingerprints.

GOING TO COURT

Once the police have collected enough evidence, the suspect goes to court. The court decides whether the suspect is guilty.

CONTROLLING TRAFFIC

Sometimes police officers need to direct and control traffic. For example, this may happen when there has been a car crash.

TEACHING THE COMMUNITY

Police officers may teach at schools and workplaces. They inform others about how to stay safe.

AT THE POLICE STATION

There are many differen rooms in police stations.

HOLDING CELLS

Suspects are kept in holding cells before they are interviewed.

INTERVIEW ROOMS

Police officers ask suspects, witnesses, or victims questions in interview rooms.

BSERVATION ROOMS

ome police stations have bservation rooms. These ooms allow other officers o see and hear what is appening in the interview ooms.

EVIDENCE STORAGE ROOM

Most police stations have a room where evidence is stored until it is needed in court.

EQUIPMENT

Police officers use different kinds of equipment to do their job.

Police cars have sirens and lights to warn people that they are coming. Police cars are fast. They may be used to chase criminals.

Police officers wear uniforms. Most wear badges. Some wear hats or helmets. Many wear bulletproof vests.

Bulletproof vest

DID YOU KNOW?
Most bulletproof vests can weigh up to 7 pounds (3 kg).

Police officers may use radios to talk to one another.

Body cameras are small cameras that police officers wear. They are attached to police uniforms. The cameras record evidence. For example, they can record officers' conversations with witnesses.

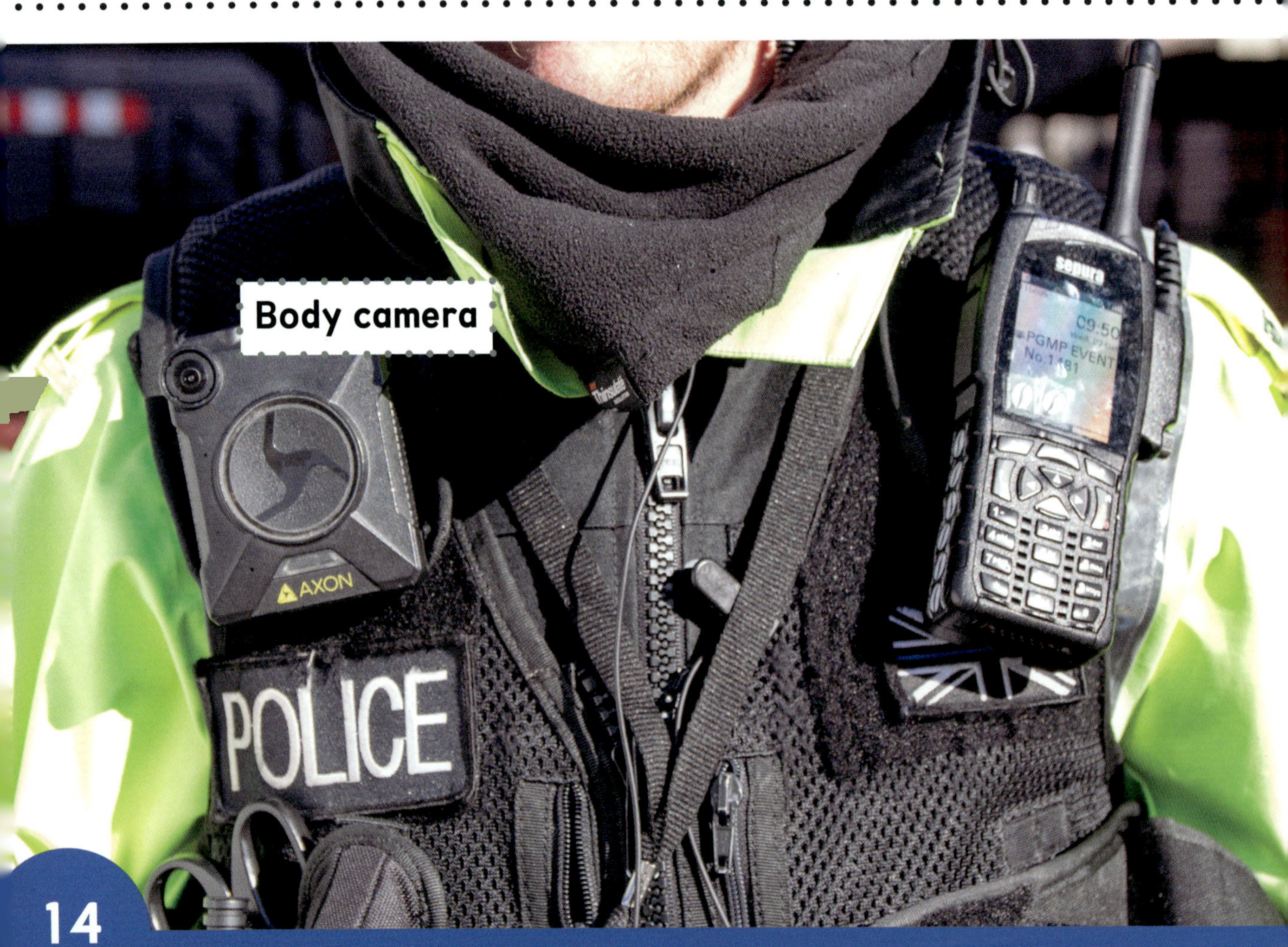

Police officers use handcuffs. Handcuffs can control people who may be dangerous.

A HISTORY OF POLICING

3000 BCE
The first organized police system was created in Egypt.

1829
The Metropolitan Police was created in London, England. Future police systems in the United States were based on this police force.

The Middle Ages, 500–1500 CE
People worked together to protect the law in their community.

The 1840s

The first detectives began working in police departments in the United States.

1968

The first 911 call was made. This number is still used today to call the fire, police, and ambulance services.

BECOMING A POLICE OFFICER

It takes a lot of training to become a police officer. Officers must pass a written test. They also must pass a medical exam. Most officers train at police academies.

Police officers need to be fit and healthy. They must be able o run fast and carry heavy things. Training to be an officer ncludes passing a fitness test.

BELIEVE IT OR NOT!

Some police officers work with dogs. Police dogs are called K-9s. Police have used bloodhounds to catch criminals.

The word *police* comes from the Greek word *polis*, which means "city."

Marie Owens was one of the first female police officers in the United States. She became a policewoman in 1891.

German shepherds are one of the most common dog breeds that police use.

ARE YOU A GENIUS KID?

Now you know so many facts about police officers. Your friends and family will be amazed! But what can you remember? Let's find out if you really are a genius kid.

Check back through the book if you are not sure.

1. Name one piece of equipment police officers use.
2. What is the word for people who break the law?
3. When was the first 911 call made?

Answers:
1. Police cars; Uniforms; Radios; Body cameras; or Handcuffs,
2. Criminals, 3. 1968.

GLOSSARY

BCE	Before Common Era, the time before the year 0
committing	carrying out an action
community	a group of people who are connected by something
court	a place where legal decisions can be made
detectives	police officers whose job is to solve crimes
equipment	items that are needed to complete a certain job
guilty	responsible for doing something wrong
victims	people who have had something bad done to them

INDEX